D0607537

Salsas, Chutneys & Relishes

Salsas, Chutneys & Relishes

Make Beautiful Gifts to Give (or Keep)

LINDA FERRARI

PRIMA PUBLISHING

PRIMA PUBLISHING, its colophon, and GOOD GIFTS FROM THE HOME are trademarks of Prima Publishing, a division of Prima Communications, Inc.

DISCLAIMER: THE EXPRESS PURPOSE OF SALSAS, CHUTNEYS & RELISHES IS TO PROVIDE SUGGESTIONS FOR A RECREATIONAL HOBBY. THE AUTHOR AND PUBLISHER DISCLAIM ANY WARRANTY OR GUARANTEE, EXPRESS OR IMPLIED, FOR ANY OF THE RECIPES OR FORMULAS CONTAINED HEREIN AND FURTHER DISCLAIM ANY LIABILITY FOR THE READER'S EXPERIMENTS OR PROJECTS. THE AUTHOR OR PUBLISHER DO NOT ASSUME ANY LIABILITY FOR ANY DAMAGES THAT MAY OCCUR AS A RESULT OF READING OR FOLLOWING ANY OF THE RECIPES OR FORMULAS IN THIS BOOK. THE PURCHASE OF THIS BOOK BY THE READER WILL SERVE AS AN ACKNOWLEDGMENT OF THIS DISCLAIMER AND AN AGREEMENT TO HOLD THE AUTHOR AND PUBLISHER HARMLESS FOR ANY MISTAKES THE READER MAY MAKE AS A RESULT OF FOLLOWING THE RECIPES AND FORMULAS IN THIS BOOK.

Library of Congress Cataloging-in-Publication Data

Ferrari, Linda.
    Salsas, chutneys & relishes / by Linda Ferrari.
        p.   cm. — (Good gifts from the home)

    Includes index.
    ISBN 0-7615-0333-1
    1. Chutney.   2. Cookery (Relishes)   3. Salsas (Cookery)
I. Title.   II. Series.
TX819.A1F47 1996   95-26067
641.8'12—dc20   CIP

96 97 98 99 00 AA 10 9 8 7 6 5 4 3 2 1

Printed in the United States of America

How to Order:
Single copies may be ordered from Prima Publishing, P.O. Box 1260BK, Rocklin, CA 95677; telephone (916) 632-4400. Quantity discounts are also available. On your letterhead, include information concerning the intended use of the books and the number of books you wish to purchase.

To the friendships I cherish and people I work with at Loaves and Fishes: Chris Delany, Lynn, Fawcett, Gene, Bob, Karen, Margaret-Mary, Augie, Chris, Jeannie, Alan, Jerry, James, David, Jewels, and the hundreds of other great people who help feed the less fortunate every day.

CONTENTS

ACKNOWLEDGMENTS

A spicy thanks to all my friends and family who tried my many salsas, chutneys, and relishes; I also thank my friend and agent Linda Hayes, the staff at Prima Publishing, and the Dunlavey Studio for helping to make this book a reality.

Cooking today embraces the use of the freshest and finest foods we can purchase. The fresh flavors of salsas, chutneys, and relishes enhance the flavors of our dishes and can make the simplest foods taste fabulous. Now, wonderful fresh vegetables and fruits are available to us all year long, and it is fashionable to make these accompaniments fresh. Innovative restaurants serve such delightful, often unique, combinations that can become the primary focus of interest in a dish.

Today's trend in cooking is the fusion of different cuisines, techniques, and ingredients to produce new, often inspired combinations of flavor. Along with taste, nutrition is a concern. The little bursts of flavor provided by chutneys, salsas, and relishes certainly add to the nutritional value and are also low in fat. These condiments can add excitement to grilled, boiled, and broiled foods and awaken our senses. I hope you will enjoy these recipes—maybe even adapt them to your own tastes, according to your own creative genius!

Tips for Creating Delicious Salsas, Chutneys, and Relishes

- Always use the freshest and ripest ingredients possible.
- Necessary equipment includes a sharp knife, a cutting board, a grinder, bowls, measuring cups and spoons, a medium-sized saucepan, and food processor (nice but not necessary) or blender.
- If you are not familiar with a particular ingredient, do not hesitate to ask your local grocer. Be adventurous when you have the time, and make substitutions when necessary.
- Use the best oils, vinegars, and spices. It is hard to hide harsh, old-tasting ingredients.
- Use fresh salsas with fruit on the day they are made. Other salsas will hold for two or three days.
- Chutneys and relishes will last refrigerated for a week or two. Before using them, bring to room temperature for optimum flavor.
- For sweeteners you can use white or brown sugar, or honey.
- Be flexible, substituting your favorite spices, fruits, or vegetables to personalize these recipes.
- To add flavor and interest you may want to plump your dried fruit in fruit juice, brandy, or your favorite liqueur.

CHAPTER ONE

Chutneys

LIKE THE salsas and relishes described in this book, our chutneys are made with fresh ingredients. This is so exciting! In this little book we will be making smaller amounts of fresh chutney, enabling us to play with ingredients, coming up with great new chutneys every time we make them. The range of possibilities when combining sweet and fruity flavors with sour, hot, and spicy flavors is limitless. Fruits, vegetables, dried fruits, and sometimes nuts are used in creative ways with spices, vinegars, and sweeteners to make these recipes really special. You will find that chutneys complement many different dishes, and your experiments can lead to delicious discoveries.

APPLE CHUTNEY

. . . .

🐌 *I am fortunate to live close to a place called "Apple Hill," a small community of apple farms. It's a delightful place to visit in September. You can buy cases of several varieties of apples while sampling delicious fritters, pies, caramel apples, wine, and many other apple delights.*

Makes about 3½ cups

    4 large Golden Delicious apples, peeled, cored, and finely chopped
    1 red pepper, seeded and finely chopped
    1 medium onion, chopped
    ⅓ cup dried blueberries
    ⅓ cup chopped crystallized ginger
    1 cup brown sugar
    ¾ cup apple cider vinegar
    Juice of 2 lemons
    1 teaspoon cinnamon
    ¼ teaspoon ground cloves
    ¼ teaspoon mace
    ½ teaspoon salt

. . . .

Put all of the ingredients into a large saucepan and cook until the apples are tender and the desired consistency has been reached. Cool the mixture and refrigerate in tightly covered containers.

APPLE–WALNUT CHUTNEY

....

Toasting the walnuts adds a distinctive touch to this chutney. Try serving this with a beautiful crown pork roast.

Makes about 3½ cups

  ½ cup walnuts, toasted
  1 onion, chopped
  1 clove garlic, minced
  2 tomatoes, peeled and diced
  1 tablespoon butter
  4 large Granny Smith apples, peeled, cored, and chopped
  2 jalapeños, minced
  ½ cup fresh apple juice
  ½ cup apple cider vinegar
  1 cup light brown sugar
  1 teaspoon *each* cinnamon, cloves, and mustard seed
  ½ cup dried cranberries
  2 tablespoons Calvados or applejack brandy

....

To toast the walnuts, put them in a dry frying pan and shake over high heat until a toasty smell arises. Set aside.

In the same frying pan, combine the onion, garlic, tomatoes, and butter; sauté until the onion softens. Transfer the mixture to a heavy saucepan, adding all of the other ingredients except the walnuts and liqueur. Cook until the apples are soft and a thick, juicy consistency has been reached. Remove the saucepan from the heat and stir in the walnuts and liqueur and let the mixture cool. Put the chutney in a container with a tight-fitting lid and refrigerate.

. . . .

Chayote are pear-shaped fruit that taste a lot like cucumbers. This recipe can be altered by substituting raisins or currants and using your favorite nuts. This chutney tastes delicious spread in a pita half that is then filled with grilled chicken.

Makes about 2½ cups

    5 chayote, finely chopped
    4 tomatillos, papery skins removed, finely chopped
    1 red bell pepper, finely chopped
    1 large onion, chopped
    ½ to 1 teaspoon crushed red pepper flakes
    ½ cup chopped dried apples
    1½ cups brown sugar
    1½ cups cider vinegar
    ½ cup water
    ⅛ teaspoon nutmeg
    ½ teaspoon *each* cloves and allspice
    1½ teaspoons cumin
    ¼ cup chopped cilantro
    ½ cup peanuts

. . . .

Combine all of the ingredients, except the peanuts, in a large, heavy saucepan and cook until soft and the desired consistency has been reached. Remove the saucepan from the heat, stir in the nuts, and let cool. Store the chutney in containers with tight-fitting lids and refrigerate.

COCONUT CHUTNEY

This is an amazing tropical chutney to serve with grilled fish or on fried salmon with a crust of fried potatoes.

Makes 4 cups

Meat from 1 coconut, grated
1 onion, chopped
3 cloves garlic, minced
1 red bell pepper, chopped
2 teaspoons olive oil
Juice of 1 lemon
½ to 1 teaspoon dried red pepper flakes
2 tablespoons minced fresh ginger
½ cup golden raisins
1 cup apple cider vinegar
½ cup sugar
1 teaspoon cinnamon
½ teaspoon *each* allspice, cloves, and cayenne pepper
¼ teaspoon salt
3 medium Granny Smith apples, peeled, cored, and chopped
2 peaches, peeled, pitted, and chopped
½ cup macadamia nuts

Buy a fresh coconut and pierce it in several places. Bake the coconut in a rimmed, oven-proof pan in a 375°F oven for 30 minutes. Using a hammer, split open the coconut. Cut away the coconut meat, rinse it, and chop or grate. Set aside.

Put the onion, garlic, pepper, and olive oil in a heavy saucepan and cook until the onion begins to soften. Add all of the other ingredients except the fruit and nuts and cook for 10 minutes. Add the apples and cook until they are tender, and then add the peaches and nuts, continuing to cook until the peaches are tender. Cool and store the mixture in a container with a tight-fitting lid. Refrigerate.

FAVORITE PAPAYA CHUTNEY

....

This chutney is a family favorite. It goes well with everything: meat, poultry, fish, and even a dab on some freshly made potato pancakes.

Makes about 2 ⅓ cups

    1 ½ cups finely chopped papaya
    ½ yellow bell pepper, finely chopped
    ½ medium onion, finely chopped
    1 serrano chili, seeded and minced
    ⅓ cup dried cranberries
    ¼ cup slivered almonds
    ½ cup light brown sugar
    ¾ cup sherry vinegar
    1 tablespoon crystallized ginger, minced
    ½ teaspoon coriander seed
    ½ teaspoon salt

Put all of the ingredients into a heavy saucepan and bring to a boil, stirring to dissolve the sugar. Lower the heat and cook until the mixture is slightly thickened and syrupy. Remove from heat and cool. Keep refrigerated in a jar with a tight-fitting lid.

....

GREENGAGE PLUM CHUTNEY

....

You will enjoy this chutney. It is not hot and spicy, but rather a mild condiment to complement spicier foods. I like to roast Cornish game hens and brush them with this chutney for the last thirty minutes.

Makes about 3 cups

> 2 pounds Greengage plums, peeled, pits removed, and finely chopped
> 1 cup fresh cranberries, washed and sorted
> 1 tablespoon finely chopped crystallized ginger
> 1 tablespoon lemon zest
> ½ cup cider vinegar
> ½ cup plus 1 tablespoon brown sugar
> ¼ teaspoon nutmeg
> ½ teaspoon cinnamon
> ½ teaspoon cardamom
> ¼ teaspoon salt
> ½ cup golden raisins, plumped in ¼ cup Grand Marnier

Put all of the ingredients in a heavy saucepan and bring to a boil, stirring to dissolve the sugar. Lower the heat and continue to cook until the mixture begins to thicken. Remove from heat and cool. Store in airtight containers in the refrigerator.

....

FIVE-PEPPER CHUTNEY

The beautiful peppers of summer make an outstanding chutney to serve with grilled meats, such as flank steak or London broil, and roasted potatoes.

Makes about 1 ¾ cups

 ½ cup toasted pine nuts
 1 yellow bell pepper, finely chopped
 1 Anaheim chili pepper, finely chopped
 1 red bell pepper, finely chopped
 1 jalapeño pepper, finely chopped
 1 serrano pepper, minced
 1 onion, chopped
 2 garlic cloves, minced
 1 tablespoon chopped fresh cilantro
 ½ cup red wine vinegar
 ¼ cup water
 ¾ cup brown sugar
 ½ teaspoon mustard seed
 1 teaspoon salt

Toast the pine nuts: put them in a small, dry frying pan, and shake over high heat until the nuts turn golden. Set aside.

Put all of the other ingredients into a heavy saucepan and cook until the vegetables are soft. Stir in the nuts and allow to cool. Refrigerate overnight before serving.

GREEN CHUTNEY

This recipe uses green tomatoes—not to be confused with tomatillos. Serving this with salmon patties makes for a delicious combination and stunning presentation.

Makes 2 ½ cups

1 leek, white part only, finely chopped
2 garlic cloves, minced
1 teaspoon olive oil
3 medium green tomatoes, peeled and finely chopped
½ green bell pepper, peeled and finely chopped
1 jalapeño, seeded and minced
1 pear, peeled, cored, and finely chopped
Juice of 1 lime
½ cup sugar
¾ cup champagne vinegar
½ teaspoon *each* cumin seed, coriander seed, and mustard seed
½ teaspoon salt
⅓ cup golden raisins
¼ cup pumpkin seed

Sauté the leek and garlic in olive oil in a heavy saucepan until the leek wilts. Add all of the other ingredients, except the pumpkin seed, and cook until the mixture is slightly thickened and syrupy. Stir in the pumpkin seed and let the mixture cool. Refrigerate in containers with tight-fitting lids.

MANGO–KIWI CHUTNEY

··

Bring this chutney as a gift when invited to dinner. It is so versatile, you can serve it with any meat, fish, or poultry dish; it will also complement your favorite turkey sandwich.

Makes about 1¾ cups

    1 teaspoon butter
    ½ medium onion, finely chopped
    ⅓ cup brown sugar
    1½ teaspoons curry powder
    ⅓ cup sherry vinegar
    1 cinnamon stick
    ½ teaspoon cayenne
    ¼ cup dried cranberries
    3 tablespoons almond slivers
    3 mangoes, peeled, seeded, and finely chopped
    4 kiwi, peeled and finely chopped

Place the butter and onion in a heavy saucepan over medium heat and stir the onion until it softens slightly. Add the sugar, curry, vinegar, cinnamon, cayenne, and cranberries. Cook the mixture for 10 minutes. Stir in the almonds, mangoes, and kiwi and cook for 3 minutes. Remove from heat and let cool. Discard the cinnamon stick and put the mixture in a container with a tight-fitting lid. Refrigerate until ready to use.

....

This combination may seem strange, but the results are excellent. Try spreading it on toasted baguette slices.

Makes almost 2 cups

> ½ cup finely chopped imported green olives, rinsed, drained, and pitted
> ½ cup finely chopped calamata olives, drained, and pitted
> ½ cup finely chopped black seedless grapes
> ½ red bell pepper, finely chopped
> 2 tablespoons finely chopped onion
> 2 cloves garlic, minced
> 1 tablespoon grapeseed oil or virgin olive oil
> 1 tablespoon orange zest
> ⅓ cup balsamic vinegar
> ¼ cup sugar
> ½ teaspoon *each* coriander seed, mustard seed, and celery seed
> ¼ teaspoon salt
> 1 teaspoon cayenne

Combine all of the ingredients in a heavy saucepan and bring to a boil. Reduce the heat and cook for 8 minutes, or until the mixture thickens and achieves the desired consistency. Remove from heat and let cool. Store in the refrigerator in tightly covered jars.

....

PURPLE PLUM CHUTNEY

....

Brown and crisp some pork ribs on the grill, and for the last fifteen minutes brush them with this delicious chutney.

Makes about 3 ½ cups

   2 pounds purple plums, peeled and finely chopped
   3 pears, peeled, cored, and finely chopped
   1 green bell pepper, finely chopped
   1 small onion, sliced into thin rings
   ¾ teaspoon crushed red pepper flakes
   ¾ teaspoon ground coriander
   ⅓ cup brown sugar
   ⅓ cup red wine vinegar
   ½ teaspoon *each* salt and black pepper
   1 tablespoon lemon zest
   ½ cup golden raisins

Combine all of the ingredients and bring to a boil, stirring to dissolve the sugar. Reduce the heat and let the mixture cook for 30 minutes, or until it has thickened slightly. Remove from heat and let cool. Store in the refrigerator in tightly covered jars.

....

PAPAYA AND CRAB APPLE CHUTNEY

🦃 *This chutney is terrific when served as a condiment with Indian cuisine.*

Makes about 2 ½ cups

⅓ cup toasted black walnuts
1 medium onion, finely chopped
1 teaspoon chili oil
2 cups peeled and finely diced papaya
1 cup cored and finely diced spiced crab apples
1 serrano chili, minced
⅓ cup light brown sugar
¼ cup balsamic vinegar
¼ cup water
½ teaspoon *each* salt, pepper, cinnamon, and nutmeg
1 teaspoon curry powder
½ cup dried cherries
3 tablespoons slivered mint

Toast the walnuts: put them in a dry frying pan and shake them over high heat until they are very fragrant. Set aside.

Combine the onion and chili oil in a heavy saucepan and cook for 1 minute. Add all of the other ingredients, except the mint and walnuts, and cook for 10 minutes. Remove from the heat and stir in the mint and nuts. Let cool and store in the refrigerator in a container with a tight-fitting lid.

PEACHY PECAN CHUTNEY

....

🔖 *Dried blueberries, dried cherries, or dried raspberries all give such great flavor to chutney. I especially like this chutney with chicken.*

Makes about 3 ½ cups

    1 pound dried peaches, finely chopped
    ⅓ cup dried blueberries
    ¼ cup Grand Marnier liqueur
    1 red bell pepper, finely chopped
    1 apple, peeled, cored, and finely chopped
    ¾ cup brown sugar
    ⅓ cup lemon juice
    ¼ cup *each* water and white wine vinegar
    2 cinnamon sticks
    ⅛ teaspoon ground cloves
    1 teaspoon *each* mustard seed and nutmeg
    ½ teaspoon cayenne
    ¼ cup finely chopped toasted pecans

....

Plump the peaches and blueberries in Grand Marnier for 1 hour.

Put all of the ingredients in a heavy saucepan, including the peach mixture. Bring the mixture to a boil, stirring well to dissolve the sugar. Reduce the heat and let it cook until the mixture begins to thicken, about 20 to 30 minutes. Remove the chutney from the heat and discard the cinnamon sticks. Let cool and put into jars with tight-fitting lids. Refrigerate.

TOMATO AND PEPPER CHUTNEY

....

Today it is hard to tell salsas, relishes, and chutneys apart. They are all relishes, technically—a combination of fruits and vegetables with sweet, sour, and spicy flavors. Many Indian chutneys are not cooked, but instead are a mixture of raw ingredients, as with this recipe. With the acidic taste of tomatoes, the spicy flavor of the peppers, and the sweetness of the pineapple, this makes for an exquisite blend of flavors. Try it with lamb dishes.

Makes about 1½ cups

  2 tomatoes, peeled, seeded, and finely diced
  1 yellow pepper, finely diced
  1 jalapeño, minced
  2 green onions, finely diced
  ½ cup finely diced fresh pineapple
  2 tablespoons dried currants
  2 tablespoons honey
  1 tablespoon cider vinegar
  ½ teaspoon *each* salt and pepper
  1 teaspoon grated fresh ginger
  1 teaspoon crushed coriander seed

....

Mix all of the ingredients together and refrigerate in a tightly covered container. This chutney will last in the refrigerator for two to three days.

CHAPTER TWO

Relishes

YESTERDAY, sauces were the main focus for many good cooks creating delicious signature dishes. Today, we can still make sauces that are simmered, strained, and reduced, as in the past, but we can also create relishes—deliciously piquant blends of fruits, vegetables, sugar, vinegar, spices, and herbs. A relish is made of fresh, chunky ingredients, so that we can still taste all of the beautiful, individual flavors. It can be sweet, sour, hot, or spicy; in fact, a relish is a lot like a salsa, only much thicker.

Many cultures have contributed to making relishes the provocative condiments they are today, and it is the fusion of cultures that makes cooking such an exciting adventure. Just remember: relishes are not just for hot dogs and hamburgers. Serve them as an accompaniment to many meats, vegetables, and appetizers.

AVOCADO–CITRUS RELISH

Use Avocado–Citrus Relish immediately for best results. I like it with boiled shrimp or crisp-fried wontons. Or try a dab of this relish topped with a grilled shrimp or scallop.

Makes about 1½ cups

⅓ cup pine nuts, toasted
2 avocados, peeled, pits removed, and finely diced
Juice and zest of 1 lemon
1 orange, peeled, divided into segments, and finely diced
3 tablespoons finely diced red onion
¼ to ½ teaspoon crushed red pepper flakes
½ teaspoon allspice
½ cup white wine vinegar
2 teaspoons sugar
1 teaspoon celery seed
Salt and pepper to taste

To toast the pinenuts, put them in a small, nonstick frying pan and shake over high heat until they turn golden. Set aside.

Combine the avocados, lemon juice and zest, and orange in a bowl and set aside. Put the pine nuts, onion, pepper flakes, allspice, vinegar, sugar and celery seed in a pan and let the mixture come to a boil. Boil for 2 minutes, stirring constantly. Let the mixture cool, then pour it into the avocado mixture. Gently mix. Salt and pepper to taste. Use immediately or refrigerate until ready to use. It's best to use it the day it is made.

BEET AND APPLE RELISH

This is a beautiful, deep-red relish. My family likes all kinds of vegetable pancakes—potato, zucchini, sweet potato, parsnip, and corn, to name a few—and it's fun to serve this relish as one of several toppings for them.

Makes about 5 half-pints

    2 pounds beets, peeled
    3 pounds apples, cored and peeled
    1 large onion, peeled
    2 tablespoons horseradish
    1 cup cider vinegar
    1 teaspoon coriander
    ½ teaspoon allspice
    ¼ teaspoon ground cloves
    ⅓ cup golden raisins
    ¾ cup sugar
    ½ teaspoon salt

Grind the beets, apples and onion together. Put them in a pan and stir in the other ingredients. Cook, stirring, until the mixture comes to a boil. Reduce the heat and cook the mixture until it thickens, about 20 minutes.

DRIED TOMATO RELISH

....

🔖 *You can use canned beans for this recipe; if you do, be sure to rinse the beans several times before using. Try serving a little Dried Tomato Relish on some fresh cooked greens.*

Makes about 1½ cups

    ½ cup chopped dried tomatoes in olive oil
    1 onion, chopped
    3 garlic cloves, minced
    1 green bell pepper, seeded
    ½ cup canned white beans
    ¼ cup sugar
    3 tablespoons lemon juice
    3 tablespoons cider vinegar
    1 tablespoon fresh oregano
    1 tablespoon slivered fresh basil
    1 teaspoon salt
    1 teaspoon white pepper

Grind the tomatoes, onion, garlic, and bell pepper in a food processor or grinder. Add all of the other ingredients and cook for 10 minutes, or until the mixture thickens.

....

CARROT AND JALAPEÑO RELISH

Use Carrot and Jalapeño Relish to enrich many dishes; it's especially good with baked ham or pork.

Makes 2 cups

> 2 cups diced carrots
> 4 shallots, peeled
> 4 plum tomatoes, peeled and left whole
> Vegetable spray
> Olive oil
> Salt and pepper to taste
> 2 jalapeños, seeded and minced
> 1 small can crushed pineapple; include the liquid
> 1 tablespoon light brown sugar
> 1/3 cup apple cider vinegar
> 1/2 teaspoon dried rosemary
> 1/4 teaspoon ground cloves

Preheat the oven to 375°F. Put the carrots, shallots, and tomatoes in a small, oven-proof pan coated with vegetable spray. Drizzle the vegetables with olive oil and sprinkle with salt and pepper. Bake in the oven for 20 minutes. Transfer the vegetables from the pan to a food processor and chop the mixture.

Combine the roasted vegetables, jalapeños, pineapple, brown sugar, vinegar, rosemary, and ground cloves in a saucepan and let the mixture come to a boil. Cook, stirring, for 2 minutes. Remove and put the relish in a container with a tight-fitting lid and refrigerate for up to two weeks.

CHIPOTLE AND RED ONION RELISH

· ·

A chipotle chili is a dried jalapeño. It is brown in color and fairly hot. If you cannot find chipotle chilies dried, you can usually find them canned. This relish is delicious stirred into mayonnaise and served on a tuna sandwich.

Makes about 1½ cups

  2 chipotle chilies
  1 red onion, quartered
  2 garlic cloves, minced
  1 green bell pepper, seeded and cut into quarters
  ½ cup corn kernels
  1 stalk celery, diced
  1 carrot, peeled and diced
  1 cup cider vinegar
  ¼ cup water
  ½ cup sugar
  1 teaspoon dry mustard
  1 teaspoon salt

If the chilies are dried (not canned), soak them in hot water to cover for 10 minutes, then purée with 2 tablespoons of the water they soaked in. Grind all of the solid ingredients in a food processor or grinder. Put the resulting mixture, along with the rest of the ingredients, in a pan and bring to a boil. Reduce the heat and let it cook for 15 minutes, until the relish thickens.

. . . .

The habanero chili is about thirty to fifty percent hotter than the jalapeño pepper. Be very careful to wear rubber gloves when mincing up habanero chilies. If you feel undaunted by the intensity of this relish, use it on beef or chicken dishes and enjoy! I love it, but then I adore fiery foods. It is also great to spread on top of a round of Brie cheese encased in puff pastry.

Makes about 1 ¼ cups

> 2 habanero chilies, halved and seeded
> 1 Anaheim green chili, halved and seeded
> 1 red bell pepper, quartered and seeded
> 1 mango, peeled, pitted, and cut in large chunks
> ½ cup honey
> ¼ cup sugar
> 1 cup rice vinegar
> 2 tablespoons lime juice
> ⅓ cup chopped fresh cilantro
> ½ teaspoon salt
> 1 teaspoon cayenne pepper

. . . .

Combine the chilies, pepper, and mango in a food processor or grinder. While grinding be careful not to inhale, as the habanero can be overpowering. Put the mixture in a saucepan and add the other ingredients. Bring to a gentle boil and cook for 15 to 20 minutes. Refrigerate for at least 1 hour before using.

DAMSON RELISH

· ·

When your plum tree produces more than you can handle, try this flavorful recipe. Make a beer batter, dip fresh mozzarella in it, and fry until crisp. Serve with this relish.

Makes about 3 cups

    8 Damson plums
    1 onion
    1 green pepper
    1 red pepper
    Zest of 1 lemon
    ½ teaspoon allspice
    ½ teaspoon ground ginger
    1 cup brown sugar
    1 cup rice vinegar
    1 teaspoon crushed red pepper flakes
    1 teaspoon curry powder
    ½ teaspoon salt

· ·

Put the plums in boiling water for a few minutes, then remove and peel. Remove the pits and chop up the plums. Finely chop the onion and peppers in a food processor or grinder. Put them, along with the plums and the other ingredients, in a saucepan over high heat. Cook the mixture for 20 minutes, stirring occasionally, or until the mixture thickens. The relish can be refrigerated in tightly covered jars or sealed and processed in a water bath for 15 minutes. Refrigerated relish will last about 1 month.

FESTIVE CRANBERRY RELISH

. . . .

🥄 *Carambola, commonly called "star fruit," is a favorite of mine. I wish more people would try them so the markets would be more likely to carry them. Not only are they delicious, but they are so beautiful thinly sliced in salads, with their perfect star shape. If the fruit is a little green, let it ripen at room temperature; if it's a little brown on the edges, cut that part off and the rest of the fruit is fine. Try this one next Thanksgiving and on turkey sandwiches the next day.*

Makes 2½ cups

   ½ cup chopped and toasted macadamia nuts
   2 cups cranberries, picked over and washed
   2 star fruit *(carambola)*
   1 whole lemon, peel and white pith removed
   1 cup sugar
   ½ teaspoon ground cloves
   1 whole cinnamon stick
   1½ teaspoons nutmeg
   1 tablespoon Grand Marnier liqueur

Put the chopped nuts in a dry, nonstick pan over meduim heat; shake the pan gently until the nuts turn golden. Set aside.

Chop the cranberries, star fruit, and lemon by hand or with a food processor. Put the fruit in a heavy saucepan and add the sugar, cloves, cinnamon stick, and nutmeg. Cook until the sugar is dissolved and the mixture thickens (this will take about 8 minutes). Discard the cinnamon stick. Remove the relish from the heat and stir in the nuts and liqueur.

GINGER PEAR RELISH

....

This refreshing relish goes well with grilled or broiled foods, like salmon steaks. It is also delicious on sweet potato cakes.

Makes about 2 cups

    4 large Anjou pears, peeled, cores removed, and quartered
    1 cup red raspberries (you can use frozen berries; if so, defrost and drain)
    1 Maui onion, chopped
    1½ tablespoons minced fresh ginger
    ½ cup sugar
    ½ cup raspberry vinegar
    Juice of 2 lemons
    1 or 2 serrano peppers, seeds removed, minced
    ⅓ cup minced mint leaves
    ½ teaspoon sesame oil

Chop or grind the fruit and onion. Put into a saucepan and add all of the other ingredients. Bring to a boil and cook for about 15 minutes, or until the mixture thickens. Store in the refrigerator in jars with tight-fitting lids.

....

MINTED HONEYDEW RELISH

This is a refreshing fusion of flavors—delicious on thinly sliced lamb.

Makes about 1 cup

    1 Maui or Vidalia onion, finely diced
    2 cups finely diced honeydew melon
    ½ to 1 teaspoon crushed red pepper flakes *or* 1 red jalapeño, minced
    2 tablespoons sugar
    2 tablespoons vinegar
    ¼ cup minced fresh mint

Mix all of the ingredients in a saucepan and cook over low heat for 2 minutes. Remove from the heat and refrigerate. Drain a little before using. It's best to use Minted Honeydew Relish the same day you make it.

. . . .

There are so many different kinds of corn relish—it seems like everyone has a favorite. This one is mine. I like to eat Great Corn Relish straight out of the jar, or added to a fried calamari salad.

Makes about 3 cups

    4 ears fresh corn
    1 red bell pepper, finely diced
    1 jalapeño pepper, minced
    1 medium onion, finely diced
    1 stalk celery, finely diced
    1 carrot, finely diced
    ⅓ cup finely diced jicama
    ½ teaspoon turmeric
    ½ teaspoon cumin
    1½ cups white wine vinegar
    1 tablespoon mustard seed
    1 tablespoon celery seed
    ½ cup sugar
    Salt and pepper to taste

. . . .

Cut the corn off the cobs.

Combine all of the ingredients in a saucepan and bring to a boil. Reduce the heat and simmer until the mixture thickens, about 20 to 30 minutes. Let the mixture cool and transfer to jars with tight-fitting lids. Store in the refrigerator for up to 1 week.

OLIVE RELISH

Using an olive pitter makes seed removal fast and easy. For a real treat, serve Olive Relish with sandwiches made with grilled eggplant, or mixed into tuna. I also like crisp, small potato pancakes topped with a dab of sour cream and a little of this relish.

Makes 1⅔ cups

½ cup green pitted Italian olives
½ cup pitted black olives
⅓ cup pitted Niçoise olives
1 red pepper, finely diced
1 tablespoon washed and drained little capers
3 tablespoons finely chopped fresh flat-leaf parsley
1 tablespoon finely chopped fresh basil
2 teaspoons sugar
2 tablespoons balsamic vinegar
3 tablespoons olive oil
Ground pepper
Salt to taste (be sure to taste, because the olives are salty)

Chop the olives to a very fine dice. If you use a food processor, do not over-process. Add red pepper, capers, parsley, basil, sugar, vinegar, olive oil, and ground pepper to taste. Blend well. Heat the mixture in a saucepan for 1 minute, just to fuse flavors. Salt to taste. Refrigerate or eat at room temperature.

RED ONION AND BLOOD ORANGE RELISH

....

↘ *The uniqueness of the blood orange lies in its color and delicious taste. This special relish, mixed with a little cream cheese and spread on toast points or toasted bagels, is fantastic.*

Makes about 1 ¾ cups

    2 red onions, finely chopped
    2 garlic cloves, minced
    1 jalapeño pepper, minced
    1 red pepper, finely chopped
    5 blood oranges, peeled, sectioned, and chopped
    2 tablespoons olive oil
    ¾ cup sugar
    1 ¼ cups cider vinegar
    2 tablespoons minced fresh basil
    1 teaspoon cardamom

Finely chop by hand, or in a food processor, the onion, garlic, peppers, and oranges. Sauté the onion, garlic, and peppers in olive oil until the onion is soft. Combine the vegetables and oranges in a saucepan over medium heat. Add the rest of the ingredients and cook uncovered on high heat, stirring occasionally until the mixture thickens, about 20 to 30 minutes.

....

. . . .

🔖 *Spark up your favorite meat or salad dressing with this enticing relish.*

Makes about 2 cups

    1 onion, finely diced
    2 cloves garlic, minced
    2 passion fruit, seeds removed and pulp scooped out
    2 cucumbers, peeled, seeded, and finely diced
    2 large tomatoes, peeled and finely chopped
    1 cup finely chopped cabbage
    1 teaspoon *each* mustard seed, coriander seed, and fennel seed
    2 teaspoons black pepper
    ½ teaspoon salt
    1 cup rice vinegar
    ⅓ cup brown sugar
    2 tablespoons La Grand Passion (passion fruit liqueur) (optional)

In a food processor or by hand, finely chop the onion, garlic, passion fruit, cucumbers, tomatoes, and cabbage; put in a pan. Add all of the other ingredients, except the passion fruit liqueur, and cook the mixture until it thickens and the vegetables are soft, about 20 to 30 minutes. Stir in the liqueur and store in tightly covered jars in the refrigerator.

. . . .

SIMPLE ONION RELISH

....

Roasting the onions gives Simple Onion Relish a rich, magnificent taste. This relish is so delicious on grilled chicken sandwiches in pita pockets, sprinkled with toasted walnuts.

Makes about 2 cups

      6 Vidalia onions, peeled and quartered
      5 cloves garlic, peeled and left whole
      3 tablespoons olive oil
      Salt and pepper
      2 cups finely chopped cabbage
      1½ cups apple cider vinegar
      ½ cup sugar
      1 tablespoon honey
      1 teaspoon *each* celery seed and mustard seed
      ½ teaspoon *each* cinnamon and nutmeg

Preheat the oven to 400°F.

   Put the onions and garlic in an oven-proof dish and sprinkle with olive oil, salt, and pepper. Roast the onion mixture, uncovered, for 20 to 30 minutes or until the vegetables are soft. Crush the onions and garlic by hand, or in a grinder or food processor. Transfer the mixture to a pan and add the rest of the ingredients. Cook the mixture over medium heat until thickened, about 40 to 50 minutes. Refrigerate the relish in jars with tight-fitting lids.

TOMATILLO RELISH

Try cutting fish into thin strips and coating them with beer batter. Fry them crisp and roll into a flour tortilla with a little Tomatillo Relish.

Makes about 2 cups

2 ears of corn
8 tomatillos, papery husks removed
2 large, ripe (but firm) peaches, peeled and pits removed
2 red jalapeños, stems and seeds removed
1 green bell pepper, seeds and stem removed
1 onion, peeled and quartered
Juice of 2 limes
1¼ cups light brown sugar
1½ cups cider vinegar
½ teaspoon *each* allspice, coriander, mace, and ground cloves
½ teaspoon salt

Remove the corn kernels from cobs.

Finely chop the tomatillos, peaches, jalapeños, bell pepper, and onion in a food processor, or through a grinder. Stir in the corn kernels. Put all of these ingredients in a saucepan and add the lime juice, brown sugar, vinegar, spices, and salt. Bring the mixture to a boil, stirring to dissolve the sugar. Lower the heat and continue to cook on medium heat, until the mixture thickens, about 20 to 25 minutes.

ZUCCHINI RELISH

....

Yet another great way to use your bumper crop of zucchini! Mix some Zucchini Relish with fresh sliced mushrooms and lay on some bib lettuce for a spicy side dish.

Makes about 3 cups

    5 medium zucchini, ends removed
    1 small celeriac, peeled and cut into quarters
    3 leeks, sprouting ends removed; use only the white part
    2 medium tomatoes, peeled, cores removed
    1 large Granny Smith apple, peeled, cored, and quartered
    2 red bell peppers, seeds removed, quartered
    1 teaspoon celery seed
    1½ teaspoons mustard seed
    ½ teaspoon ground cloves
    ½ teaspoon turmeric
    2 cups rice vinegar
    1⅓ cups sugar
    ½ teaspoon salt

Grind or chop in a food processor the zucchini, celeriac, leeks, tomatoes, and apple. Combine in a large pan and add all of the other ingredients. Bring to a boil, stirring to dissolve the sugar. Reduce the heat to medium and cook until the mixture thickens, about 30 to 35 minutes. Store in jars with tight-fitting lids and refrigerate up to 2 weeks.

CHAPTER THREE

Salsas

SALSAS ARE among the most exciting condiments today. They are a fresh combination of cool, hot, sweet, and acidic flavors and textures in an array of crunchy, colorful ingredients. Some salsas are sweet and sour mixtures, some have pungent and subtle flavors, while some are cool and hot at the same time. One of the following salsa recipes combines cool watermelon and hot jalapeño—a fantastic fusion of flavors.

When making salsa, use the freshest of ingredients. Some of the recipes require cooking, but most involve combining raw foods with different tastes and textures. I like to cut all my ingredients in very fine uniform dice; this way all the flavors will fit on one spoonful, and you'll be able to taste everything at once.

If you worry about the heat in these salsas, you can downplay it by using honey, tomato paste, cooked beans, fruits, or vegetables such as peeled and seeded cucumber, jicama, or potato. If you would rather intensify the taste, do it by adding fruit juice, vinegar, chilies, cilantro, or lemon grass.

This little book is exciting because it adds fun and frivolity to our cooking and dining experience.

CACTUS SALSA

· ·

🔪 *I first tried Cactus Salsa in San Antonio, and couldn't wait to try making it at home. I love this salsa on a thick, grilled hamburger served on a baguette.*

Makes about 2½ cups

    1 large Anaheim chili pepper, diced
    2 small jalapeño peppers, seeds removed, minced
    ½ pound cactus leaves, needles and fine quills removed
    2 tomatillos, husks removed, diced
    2 green onions, diced
    2 cloves garlic, minced
    ¼ cup chopped cilantro
    ¼ cup limeade concentrate or orange juice concentrate
    ¼ teaspoon *each* salt and pepper

Prepare the peppers and transfer them to a bowl. Put the cactus into boiling water for 1 minute and plunge into cold water. Drain and dice. Add to the peppers. Add the tomatillos, onions, garlic, and cilantro and toss together. Mix in as much of the limeade as you like and season with salt and pepper to taste.

· ·

CANTALOUPE SURPRISE SALSA

This salsa is fabulous wrapped in a flour tortilla with shredded pork or stuffed in a pita pocket with pork tenderloin or chicken.

Makes about 3 to 3½ cups

2 cups small diced cantaloupe, peeled and seeded
2 green onions, diced
1 yellow bell pepper, diced small
1 tomato, peeled and diced small
1 large jalapeño pepper, seeded and minced
½ cup cooked black beans; if canned, rinse and drain
1½ tablespoons olive oil
1 tablespoon lemon juice
1½ teaspoons Dijon mustard
1 garlic clove, minced
1 tablespoon fresh thyme
1 tablespoon slivered fresh mint
Salt and pepper to taste

Dice the cantaloupe, green onions, bell pepper, and tomato very small; seed and mince the jalapeño pepper. Put all of the fruit and vegetables, along with the beans, in a bowl. Set aside.

In another small bowl whisk together the olive oil, lemon juice, mustard, and garlic and toss with the cantaloupe mixture. Gently toss in the fresh thyme and mint and season to taste with salt and pepper.

COOKED TOMATO SALSA

．．

This is a basic salsa—a favorite with tortilla chips or on omelets.

Makes 3½ cups

    1 medium onion, diced
    4 garlic cloves, minced
    3 jalapeño peppers, seeded and minced
    1 yellow pepper, finely diced
    2 tablespoons oil
    4 whole tomatoes, finely diced
    ⅓ cup tomato juice
    1 teaspoon *each* chili powder and cumin
    ½ cup chopped fresh cilantro
    2 green onions, sliced thin
    1 tablespoon red wine vinegar
    Salt and freshly ground pepper to taste

Put the onion, garlic, jalapeño, and yellow pepper in a frying pan along with the oil and cook until the onion is soft. Add the tomatoes, tomato juice, and other ingredients and let the mixture cook for 5 minutes. Remove the pan from the heat and let cool. Refrigerate until ready to use.

．．

FRESH AVOCADO SALSA

....

➴ *Use Fresh Avocado Salsa on burgers, quesadillas, or chips. It is fabulous.*

Makes about 3 cups

    2 ripe avocados
    1 tomato, seeded and diced
    1 yellow bell pepper, diced
    2 green onions, diced
    1 jalapeño chili, seeded and minced
    2 tablespoons lemon juice
    1 tablespoon virgin olive oil
    ¼ cup chopped fresh cilantro
    2 tablespoons chopped fresh parsley
    Salt to taste
    1 teaspoon cracked black pepper
    4 slices of bacon, diced, then fried and drained

Peel the avocados and remove the seeds. Dice the avocados and put them in a bowl. Add the tomato, yellow bell pepper, green onions, and chili to the avocados. Add the other ingredients and toss carefully to blend the flavors. Season to taste with salt and pepper and gently toss in the bacon. Do not mash up avocado—you want this to look chunky and beautiful.

....

GAZPACHO SALSA

If you love gazpacho soup you will think this is a delightful salsa. I love it with homemade tortilla chips or a grilled white fish.

Makes about 3 cups

> 8 ounces canned tomatoes, chopped, with juice
> 1 large red tomato, peeled, seeded, and diced
> 1 red onion, chopped
> 1 large garlic clove, minced
> 1 green pepper, diced
> 1 jalapeño, seeded and minced
> ½ cup peeled, seeded, and diced cucumber
> ¼ cup chopped cilantro or basil
> 2 tablespoons red wine vinegar
> 1 tablespoon olive oil
> ½ teaspoon Worcestershire sauce
> Salt and freshly ground pepper to taste

Put the tomatoes, onion, garlic, pepper, jalapeño, cucumber, and cilantro or basil into a bowl. In another small bowl whisk together the vinegar, oil, and Worcestershire sauce and blend well. Toss with the tomato mixture and season to taste with salt and pepper.

HAWAIIAN SALSA

....

⚓ *Hawaiian Salsa should be served immediately. It's terrific on grilled fish or chicken. I also like to serve this salsa with deep-fried wontons stuffed with shrimp or scallops. One banana, finely diced and sprinkled with lemon juice, can be added to this recipe, or substitute it for the lychee nuts.*

Makes 3½ cups

    1 cup finely diced fresh pineapple
    ½ cup finely diced kiwi
    ½ cup drained and finely diced lychee nuts
    1 green bell pepper, finely chopped
    ¼ cup finely diced red onion
    1 red jalapeño, minced
    ⅓ cup shredded fresh coconut
       (see page 9 for helpful instructions)
    ¼ cup minced macadamia nuts
    1 tablespoon vegetable oil
    2 tablespoons passion fruit liqueur

Mix all of the ingredients carefully, tossing lightly. Let the salsa sit for 15 minutes to blend the flavors before serving.

....

GRILLED VEGETABLE SALSA

....

🌿 *Grilling the vegetables gives this salsa an impressive taste. Thai basil tastes like basil with a slight anise flavor; if you can't find it substitute plain basil. Serve this with jumbo shrimp, chicken, or meatballs.*

Makes 3 to 4 cups

    1 yellow bell pepper
    1 Japanese eggplant
    1 small zucchini
    1 small onion
    1 tomato, cut in half and seeded
    1 jalapeño chili
    1 serrano chili, minced
    2 fresh pineapple rings, each ½ inch thick
    3 tablespoons olive oil
    ⅓ cup slivered Thai basil
    Juice from 2 limes
    1½ teaspoons sesame oil
    Salt and pepper to taste

....

Cut the pepper in half and remove the seeds. Cut the ends off the eggplant and zucchini and then cut each into four lengthwise strips. Peel the onion and cut it in half. Put the tomato, pepper, eggplant, zucchini, onion, jalapeño, serrano chili, and pineapple into a bowl. Pour in the olive oil and toss to coat. Next, fire up the barbecue, or turn on the indoor grill, bringing it to high heat. Coat the grill with vegetable spray (e.g., Pam) and then grill the vegetables and fruit. When the yellow pepper has blackened somewhat, put it in a sealable plastic bag and let it sit for 10 minutes. Continue grilling the other vegetables and fruit until grill marks appear; this will take about 5 to 10 minutes, depending on how hot the grill is. Remove the vegetables and fruit and dice them all very small, discarding the chili seeds if a milder salsa is desired. Take the yellow bell pepper from its plastic bag and remove the skin with a knife. Now dice the pepper and add it to the other vegetables. Sprinkle with basil, lime juice, and sesame oil and toss gently. Season to taste with salt and pepper.

ITALIAN SALSA

....

Serve Italian Salsa with thin slices of veal or turkey. Canned fire-roasted peppers are available in most grocery stores. If you can't find them, then char a red pepper, peel, and dice.

Makes almost 2 cups

    1 medium green zucchini
    1 medium yellow zucchini
    1 leek, white part only, minced
    2 cloves garlic, minced
    1 tablespoon virgin olive oil
    1 fire-roasted red pepper, peeled and chopped
    ¼ cup pitted and diced black olives
    1 tablespoon washed and drained tiny capers
    2 tablespoons chopped flat-leaf parsley
    Juice of 1 lemon
    2 tablespoons virgin olive oil
    Salt and pepper to taste

In a 10-inch skillet combine the green and yellow zucchini, leek, garlic, and olive oil and sauté for 2 to 3 minutes, until the vegetables just begin to soften. Add the red pepper, olives, and capers and mix well. Transfer the mixture from the skillet to a bowl and add the other ingredients; toss together. This salsa is best when served at room temperature.

....

This is a superb, crunchy salsa with an exotic sweetness from the Persian melon and figs. To seed the tomatoes, cut their tops off, turn them upside down, and squeeze. Serve Jicama and Chili Salsa with anything crispy: deep-fried chicken pieces, fish pieces, shrimp, or vegetables.

Makes about 3 cups

   1 medium jicama, peeled and diced
   1 large Anaheim chili, seeded and diced
   1 red jalapeño chili, seeded and minced
   2 tomatoes, seeds removed, diced
   1 yellow pepper, diced
   1 cup diced Persian melon
   4 figs, peeled and chopped
   3 green onions, sliced
   1 clove garlic, minced
   1 tablespoon fresh lemon thyme
   ¼ cup rice vinegar
   1 tablespoon walnut oil
   2 tablespoons tequila (optional)
   Salt and pepper

....

In a bowl combine the jicama, chilies, tomatoes, pepper, melon, figs, onions, garlic, and lemon thyme. Whisk together the vinegar, oil, and tequila (if desired); toss carefully with the jicama mixture. Season to taste with salt and pepper.

MANGO–PECAN SALSA

Try Mango–Pecan Salsa on grilled meat, fish, or poultry; another time intrigue your guests with a goat cheese (or fresh mozzarella) salad topped with this special salsa.

Makes about 3 cups

> 3 tablespoons toasted pecans, chopped
> 1 small jicama, peeled and diced
> 2 small mangoes, pitted, peeled, and diced
> 2 ripe but firm peaches, peeled, pitted, and finely diced
> 1 small green bell pepper, seeded and diced small
> 1 red jalapeño, seeded and minced
> 2 tablespoons slivered mint leaves
> 1 tablespoon walnut oil
> ¼ cup orange juice
> 1 teaspoon light brown sugar
> Salt and pepper to taste

Toast the pecans: put them in a dry skillet in a 350°F oven, stirring occasionally, until the nuts are fragrant and taste toasted. This takes about 10 to 15 minutes.

In a bowl combine the pecans with the jicama, mangoes, peaches, pepper, jalapeño, and mint. Whisk together the oil, orange juice, and brown sugar and blend well. Toss this with the other ingredients and season to taste with salt and pepper.

MEDITERRANEAN SALSA

....

🌿 *Mediterranean Salsa enriches the flavor of many dishes. Try it on cold pasta for a summer salad.*

Makes about 2 cups

   1 medium Portobella mushroom, cleaned and diced small
   1 cup diced small button mushrooms
   1 large tomato, seeded and diced
   2 garlic cloves, minced
   2 tablespoons minced onion
   10 Niçoise olives, pitted and chopped
   2 tablespoons *each* chopped fresh basil and fresh parsley
   1 tablespoon lemon juice
   1 tablespoon balsamic vinegar
   ¼ to 1 teaspoon red pepper flakes
   2 tablespoons olive oil
   Salt to taste
   1 to 2 teaspoons fresh cracked black pepper

In a bowl, combine the mushrooms, tomato, garlic, onion, olives, basil, and parsley. Whisk together the other ingredients and toss with the mushroom mixture.

....

NECTARINE SALSA

Be sure you use ripe nectarines for this tasty salsa, which is delicious on fresh tuna or pork tenderloin. Dice everything very small to make a really nice combination.

Makes about 3 cups

> 1½ pounds nectarines, diced (I leave the skins on for texture)
> 1 cup fresh raspberries
> 3 tablespoons diced Vidalia onion
> 1 jalapeño, seeded and minced
> 2 tablespoons pine nuts
> 1 garlic clove, minced
> 2 tablespoons chopped fresh cilantro
> 1 tablespoon raspberry vinegar
> 1 tablespoon Chambord
> 2 teaspoons olive oil
> Salt and pepper to taste

Combine the nectarines, raspberries, onion, jalapeño, pine nuts, garlic, and cilantro in a bowl. In another bowl whisk together all of the remaining ingredients. Sprinkle the dressing carefully over the fruit and vegetable mixture. Let the salsa stand for 20 minutes to blend flavors. This salsa should be both sweet and pungent; if it's too sweet add a little more vinegar.

PUNGENT PAPAYA SALSA

....

🔖 *Pungent Papaya Salsa has a very fiery burst of flavor. Serve this salsa with roasted duck, or tuck some inside a burrito made with duck meat. It will taste very special.*

Makes about 3½ cups

  1 red onion, diced small
  2 large papayas, fully ripe and diced
  1 mango, diced
  1 cup finely diced daikon radish
  2 red jalapeño peppers
  2 tablespoons chopped fresh cilantro
  1 to 2 tablespoons honey
  Juice of 1 lemon
  2 tablespoon orange juice
  ½ teaspoon cumin
  1 teaspoon cayenne
  ¼ cup shelled and roasted pumpkin seeds
  Salt to taste
  Freshly ground pink peppercorns to taste

....

In a bowl combine the onion, papayas, mango, radish, jalapeños, and cilantro. In another bowl mix the honey, lemon juice, orange juice, cumin, and cayenne. Pour this over the papaya mixture and toss lightly. Toss in the pumpkin seeds and season with salt and pepper to taste.

SOUTHERN SALSA WITH BLACK-EYED PEAS

....

🌿 *This salsa is great with pork tenderloin. It's so good you can eat it alone as a side dish. I like to grill the corn, rubbed with corn oil, and then remove the kernels — prepared this way, the corn has a wonderful smoky flavor. But if it's too much trouble, you can use canned corn, rinsed, and add ⅛ teaspoon Liquid Smoke to the salsa.*

Makes about 2½ cups

  1 fresh ear of corn, cleaned and scraped
  1 cup black-eyed peas; if canned, rinse and drain
  1 large red bell pepper, diced small
  1 or 2 jalapeños, minced
  ⅓ cup finely diced red onion
  1 teaspoon cumin
  3 tablespoons minced fresh basil
  2 tablespoons champagne vinegar
  1 tablespoon corn oil
  1 teaspoon honey
  Salt and pepper to taste

In a bowl combine the corn, black-eyed peas, pepper, jalapeño, red onion, cumin, and basil. In another bowl mix all of the other ingredients; toss gently with the corn mixture. Let sit for at least an hour in the refrigerator to blend flavors.

....

STRAWBERRY–MANGO SALSA

This hot and cool combination is terrific on a variety of meats and spinach salads.

Makes 3 cups

    1 pint strawberries, hulled and diced
    1 ripe mango, peeled and diced
    1 cucumber, peeled, seeded, and diced
    ½ to 1 teaspoon slightly crushed red pepper flakes
    3 green onions, diced
    2 tablespoons slivered fresh mint
    1 tablespoon minced fresh lemon verbena
    2 teaspoons honey, or to taste
    2 tablespoons lime juice
    1 tablespoon rum
    Salt to taste

In a bowl combine the strawberries, mango, cucumber, red pepper flakes, onions, mint, and lemon verbena. Mix the honey, lime juice, and rum in another bowl. Pour this over the strawberry mixture and toss carefully. Season to taste by adding salt, more lime juice, or honey, depending on the ripeness of the fruit. Let this salsa sit for at least 30 minutes to blend flavors.

TOMATILLO AND SPINACH SALSA

🔖 *Try wrapping this salsa in a warm flour tortilla with shredded chicken, beef, or pork.*

Makes 3 cups

  1 head garlic, roasted
  Olive oil
  Salt and pepper
  8 tomatillos, husks removed, grilled
  1 red bell pepper, grilled, skin removed, and finely diced
  2 tablespoons finely diced red onion
  2 ripe firm pears, peeled and diced
  1 serrano chili, seeded and finely diced
  2 tablespoons finely chopped fresh cilantro
  8 fresh spinach leaves, slivered
  2 tablespoons lime juice
  ¼ teaspoon hot chili paste, or to taste
  Salt and fresh ground pepper
  Pinch of sugar

First, roast the garlic. Preheat the oven to 325°F. Cut the top off a head of garlic and put the garlic in a special garlic roaster or a custard cup and drizzle with olive oil. Sprinkle with salt and pepper, cover, and roast in the oven for 1 hour and 15 minutes. Remove and let cool.

Grill the tomatillos and red pepper. Let cool and dice finely. In a bowl combine them with the onion, pears, serrano chili, cilantro, and spinach.

In another bowl whisk together the lime juice, chili paste, and roasted garlic. Toss with the tomatillo mixture and season to taste with salt, pepper, and sugar. Adjust the flavor by adding a little more lime juice if necessary.

TOMATO MINT SALSA

I hope you can find yellow tomatoes; they look gorgeous in Tomato Mint Salsa. This salsa is great served on crusted sea scallops, or any crusted food.

Makes 2½ cups

  1½ pounds yellow tomatoes, seeded and diced
  ¼ cup finely diced red bell pepper
  2 jalapeño peppers, minced
  ⅓ cup peeled, seeded, and finely diced cucumber
  1 orange, peeled, sectioned, and diced
  2 tablespoons chopped fresh chives
  2 tablespoons orange juice
  2 tablespoons minced mint leaves
  Salt and pepper to taste
  Pinch of sugar

Toss together all of the ingredients. Refrigerate and let the flavors fuse for 30 minutes.

TOMATO-RASPBERRY SALSA

⚜ *The blending of tomato and raspberry makes this salsa a surprisingly luscious treat. If you can get fresh, vine-ripened tomatoes, then this salsa will be to die for. Try it on quesadillas.*

Makes 2 cups

　1 Vidalia or Maui onion, finely diced
　3 tomatoes, seeded and finely diced
　1 yellow pepper, seeded and finely diced
　1 poblano chili
　1 tablespoon raspberry vinegar
　2 tablespoons chopped fresh cilantro
　2 teaspoons walnut oil
　Salt and pepper to taste
　1 cup chopped fresh raspberries, including juice

Toss together the onion, tomatoes (to seed the tomatoes, remove their tops, turn them upside down, and squeeze out the seeds), pepper, chili, vinegar, cilantro, and oil. Season with salt and pepper. Now: carefully mix in the raspberries and juice. Let the salsa stand for 20 minutes to blend flavors. If it's too juicy when ready to serve, drain out a little of the juice and enjoy.

WATERMELON SALSA

....

Absolutely, this is my favorite salsa. With the coolness of watermelon and the heat of the jalapeños, this is the best. Try it on grilled sea bass or halibut, or top a calamari salad with it. I am sure you will discover hundreds of uses for Watermelon Salsa.

Makes 2⅓ cups

    2 cups finely diced watermelon
    1 to 2 jalapeños, minced (suit your taste; I like it hot with the cool melon)
    2 tablespoons finely diced red onion
    2 tablespoons chopped fresh cilantro
    1 tablespoon chopped flat-leaf parsley
    ⅛ teaspoon freshly grated ginger (optional)
    ½ teaspoon *each* salt and pepper

Carefully mix everything together and let sit for 30 minutes to blend flavors. Best when used within a few hours of making.

....

WHITE BEAN SALSA

⚔ *Try serving this winning salsa on thinly sliced and toasted baguette pieces, or on grilled or fried polenta.*

Makes 2½ cups

> 1 (12 ounce) can white beans, rinsed and drained
> 2 tomatoes, seeded and finely diced
> 2 large white mushrooms, finely diced
> 10 green grapes, finely chopped
> 2 green onions, minced
> 1 clove garlic, minced
> A sprinkle of virgin olive oil
> 2 tablespoons sherry
> 1 tablespoon minced fresh tarragon
> Salt and pepper to taste

Mix all of the ingredients together and toss. Let the salsa sit for 20 minutes to blend flavors.

CHAPTER FOUR

Gift Wrapping

THESE CHUTNEY, relish, and salsa recipes require the use of fresh ingredients, and will last for one week to one month when refrigerated. They are very easy to prepare and make wonderful house gifts. Wouldn't it be wonderful if someone showed up at your next party with a tray of delicious fried wontons, stuffed with shrimp and dried tomato, accompanied by a delicious and refreshing watermelon salsa? Watermelon Salsa, like the other recipes in this book, will delight any hostess, and makes a delectable gift for any occasion.

Whether for a birthday, Mother's Day, the Fourth of July, or just as a thank-you to a friend or acquaintance, taking the time to make one of these delicious gifts will make the recipient feel special.

I have one friend who, every once in a while, leaves a surprise gift at my doorstep. I am always so excited when I return home and see a pretty basket or decorated gift bag waiting for me at my door. There doesn't have to be a reason—she just lets me know that she is thinking about me. That is a nice feeling, especially now, when we are all too busy to do the little niceties that we would like to do. The recipes in this book are quick to make, and I would like to give you a few ideas for presentation when giving them as gifts to make someone you know feel special.

The simplest way to give these delights is to place them in pretty, decorative jars. These jars can be used over and over again, making them useful as well as pretty. The jars should be labeled with either self-adhesive, decorative labels or with hanging labels that give the name of the condiment, the date it was made, and (on the backside of the label) a few ideas about how to use the gift (e.g., you might write "serve with grilled fish or roasted pork"). This is really very helpful because the recipient of your gift may not know how some recipes can be used; people are still realizing that relishes are not just for hot dogs, but can add intrigue to all kinds of meats and appetizers.

The jars can be decorated, if desired, with raffia, ribbons, or dried herbs and flowers, or topped with burlap circles that have been cut with pinking shears and tied around the tops of the jars.

Another simple way to present these gifts is to put them into small, brown paper bags that have carrying handles; if you're including more than one jar, nestle them in a pretty kitchen towel or shredded colored tissue. You can then write ways to use this goodie on a tag and, if you like, enclose the recipe for your chutney, relish, or salsa in the bag. It would also be nice to fill a basket with a few jars of a condiment, and include all the raw ingredients along with the recipe or a copy of this book. That way, they can have the fun of making some themselves while trying all the other recipes. This just may lead to your finding a treat at *your* door someday!

You could also put several different condiments in a basket or pretty box, adding cute bowls and serving spoons. There are so many pretty, colorful southwestern-style bowls, not to mention crystal, wood, and terra cotta bowls, that would make stunning additions to your basket.

A sombrero made of pottery or a straw one with a plastic insert in the top (meant to hold sauce) would be great fun to give with a salsa. You could prepare a large basket with one or more salsas, and include chips, toasted bread points, or maybe some crackers and cream cheese. Or try filling the basket with a few beers or the makings for a margarita, to go along with the salsa and chips—lots of people would enjoy that.

If you are thinking about making these treasures as Wedding, Christmas, birthday, housewarming, or thank-you gifts—that is, a bit more substantial—I can offer a few more ideas. A group of small-to-large mixing bowls is always useful, and you can nestle different relishes and chutneys in each bowl. A beautiful crystal sauce boat is an elegant way to serve these recipes, and makes for a very nice presentation of your gift. Hang small silver spoons from jars; or if you are lucky enough to have a local pottery shop, look for little jars, inscribed with "SALSA" on the front, that have a spoon attached to their sides.

Kitchen shops now sell terra cotta bakers for garlic (that would go well with the Tomatillo and Spinach Salsa) and terra cotta vegetable/onion roasters (useful when making Carrot and Jalapeño Relish or Simple Onion Relish). Giving these utensils along with the condiments makes your gift extra-special.

When you decide which items you will include in your gift, then the fun begins as you think of innovative ways of putting it all together. You can wrap boxes, fill bags, or arrange baskets to create the look you want. When using baskets you can wrap them with colored or clear cellophane, and gather and tie the ends together with ribbon, raffia, or pretty fabric. Another way to decorate a basket is to thread dried oranges, limes, lemons, apples, small red chilies, or herbs and string them like a garland hanging across the handle of the basket. I like using natural-looking adornments, such as berries, nuts, stalks of wheat, pine cones, and pine needles.

Now that you have taken the time to make these wonderful treats, and have thought of creative and original ways to decorate them, something magical may happen—you might find your friends inspired to make homemade gifts as well!

Jams, Jellies & Preserves

Linda Ferrari

Linda Ferrari shares the secrets of canning the perfect jams, jellies, and preserves as well as innovative ideas for wrapping and packaging so that anyone you present them to will feel charmed, flattered, and loved! Includes recipes for Frangelico Fig Jam, Pomegranate–Kiwi Jelly, Currant and Quince Jam, and Old-Fashioned Blackberry Preserves.

Oils, Lotions & Other Luxuries

Kelly Reno

*W*hile the luxuries made from these recipes are tempting enough to keep, they are made with friends, family, and loved ones in mind. Kelly Reno includes ideas for gorgeous wraps, packaging, and presentation. Includes recipes for Five-Oil Massage Blend, Vanilla Body Lotion, Rose Bath Beads, and Herbs and Fruit Dusting Powder.

Soaps, Shampoos & Other Suds

Kelly Reno

*I*magine the most simple ingredients—herbs, flowers, and pure soaps. Kelly Reno shows you how to work magic with these natural basics and turn them into indulgent treasures. These are simple, yet divine recipes made from the freshest ingredients. Includes recipes for Coffee and Cream Soap, Georgia Peach Shower Gel, and Peppermint Clarifying Shampoo.